Generously Donated by the

MEMPHIS LIBRARY FOUNDATION

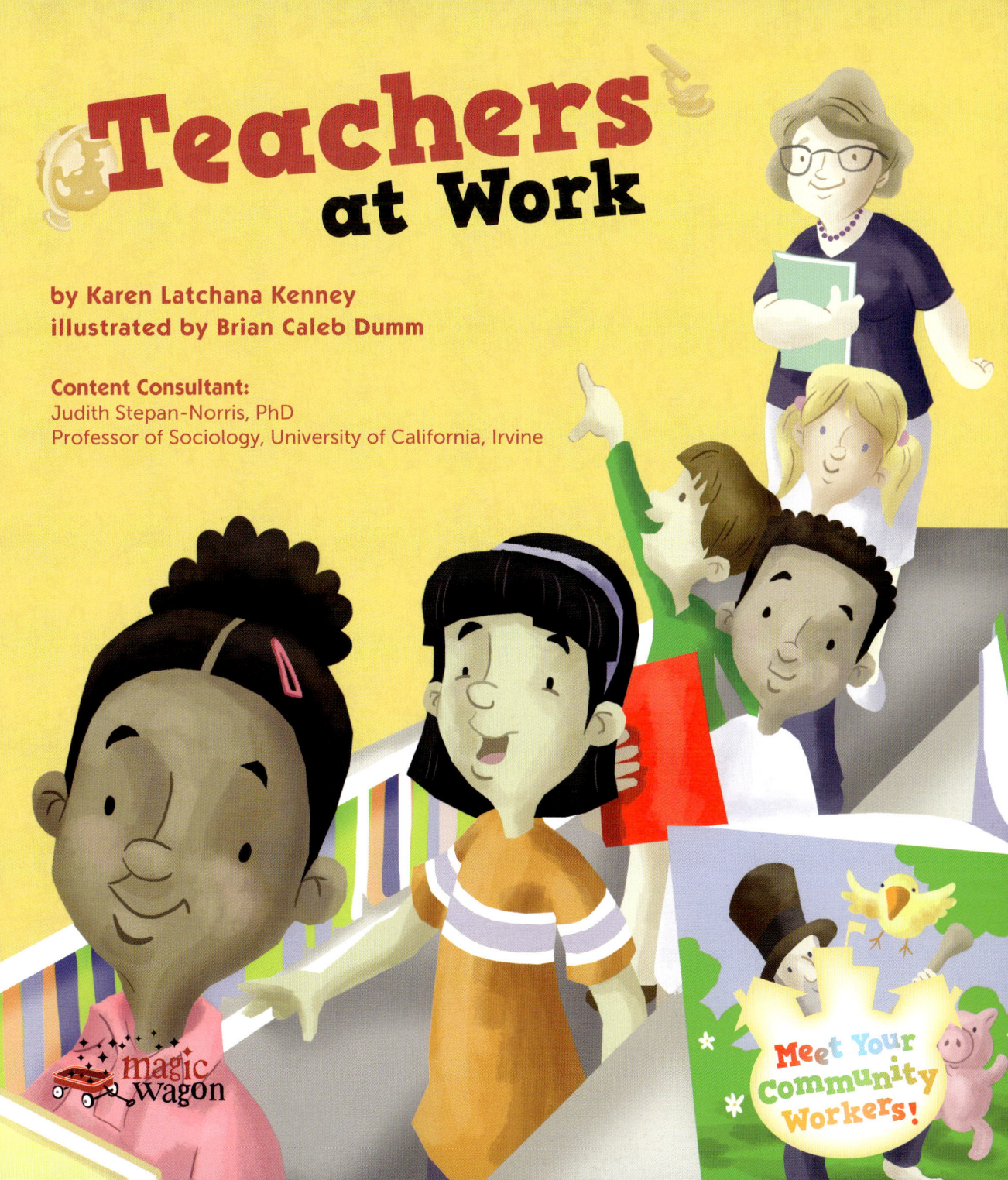
Teachers at Work

by Karen Latchana Kenney
illustrated by Brian Caleb Dumm

Content Consultant:
Judith Stepan-Norris, PhD
Professor of Sociology, University of California, Irvine

visit us at www.abdopublishing.com

Published by Magic Wagon, a division of the ABDO Group, 8000 West 78th Street, Edina, Minnesota 55439. Copyright © 2010 by Abdo Consulting Group, Inc. International copyrights reserved in all countries. All rights reserved. No part of this book may be reproduced in any form without written permission from the publisher.

Looking Glass Library™ is a trademark and logo of Magic Wagon.

Printed in the United States.
 Manufactured with paper containing at least 10% post-consumer waste

Text by Karen Latchana Kenney
Illustrations by Brian Caleb Dumm
Edited by Patricia Stockland
Interior layout and design by Emily Love
Cover design by Emily Love

Library of Congress Cataloging-in-Publication Data

Kenney, Karen Latchana.
  Teachers at work / by Karen L. Kenney ; illustrated by Brian Caleb Dumm ; content consultant, Judith Stepan-Norris.
      p. cm. — (Meet your community workers)
   Includes index.
   ISBN 978-1-60270-653-8
  1. Teachers—Juvenile literature. I. Dumm, Brian Caleb. II. Title.
LB1775.K46 2009
   371.1—dc22
                        2009002395

Table of Contents

Being a Teacher 4
Helping Others 8
At Work 11
Problems on the Job 15
Tools Teachers Need 16
Technology at Work 20
Special Skills and Training 24
In the Community 28
A Day as a Teacher 30
Glossary 31
Did You Know? 31
On the Web 32
Index 32

Being a Teacher

Did you learn something new today? Teachers help students in a class learn new things every day. Students learn to read, write, and do math problems. They also learn about science, history, and the world.

Teachers plan how to teach things to students. They teach skills and facts that students need to know. Teachers give homework and make tests. They grade students' work. They also write report cards.

Helping Others

There are different kinds of students. Some do not speak English. Some learn slowly, and others learn quickly. Teachers think of different ways to help every kind of student. Different ways of teaching help different students learn.

For example, some teachers use sign language. Students who are hearing impaired use these hand symbols to communicate and learn.

At Work

Teachers work in schools. They are in charge of a classroom of students. Teachers make rules for the class. Students need to follow the rules. Teachers also meet with the parents of students. At these meetings, or conferences, a teacher talks about a student's work.

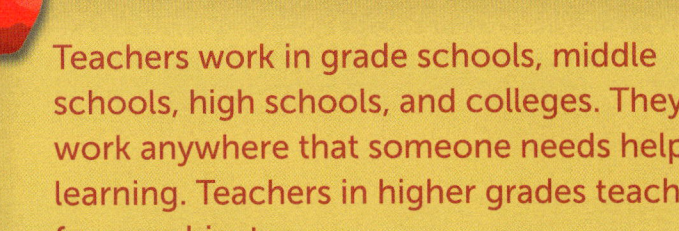

Teachers work in grade schools, middle schools, high schools, and colleges. They work anywhere that someone needs help learning. Teachers in higher grades teach fewer subjects.

A school has lots of teachers. Some teach music and art. Physical education teachers show students ways to exercise. A principal is in charge of the whole school. Teachers work with the principal to decide what to teach.

In some schools, a teacher only helps students who do not speak English.

Problems on the Job

Teachers have to keep order in the class. Sometimes students do not follow rules. It can be hard for teachers to teach those students.

Some teachers have many students in a class. Certain students need special attention. The teacher might not have time to help those students.

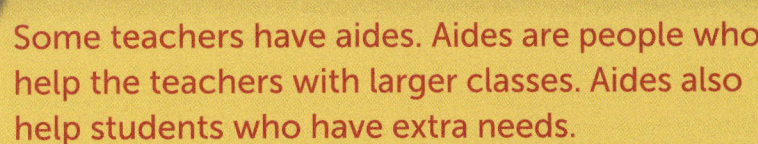

Some teachers have aides. Aides are people who help the teachers with larger classes. Aides also help students who have extra needs.

Tools Teachers Need

Books are very important tools for teachers. Students learn about different subjects by reading. They write reports about what they learn. Books also help students learn how to read, write, and spell. Because of this, libraries are important tools for teachers and students.

Science teachers need special tools, such as beakers and thermometers. These tools help students with experiments.

Games are another good way to teach students. Teachers use songs and dances to teach. Art projects are also fun teaching tools. Sometimes teachers show movies in class. Teachers use these different tools to keep classes fun.

Art teachers use special supplies such as paints, brushes, and modeling clay.

Technology at Work

Teachers use DVD or VCR players to play movies. A television or video screen shows the movies. Teachers also use overhead projectors. A projector shows things on a big screen.

Computers are very important in a classroom. Students look up information on the Internet. They play computer games that help them learn. Teachers use computers to record grades. Computers also help teachers make their teaching plans for the year. Teachers use electronic whiteboards too.

Special Skills and Training

Teachers have to love working with kids. They need to speak and listen well. They must be good at explaining things. They also need to be patient. Sometimes it can take awhile for students to understand.

Many teachers belong to unions. Unions help workers get fair pay and good working conditions.

A person has to go to school to become a teacher. In school, a person practices teaching. Then the person takes a test to become a teacher. If they pass the test, they get a license. A teacher needs to have a license to teach. Licensed teachers continue to take classes. The classes help teachers be good at their jobs.

In the Community

What have you learned from a teacher? Students learn skills that help them in a community. Teachers give students knowledge about the world around them. Teachers are an important part of every community.

A Day as a Teacher

Morning

Prepare the classroom for the day at 7:30 AM.
Welcome students to class.
Take attendance.
Explain what will happen today.
Teach students how to spell and do math.

Late Morning

Send students to art class.
Make some teaching plans.
Teach students how to read.

Afternoon

Play a science game.
Show students a science movie.
Ask students to research facts on the computer.
Grade papers.
Send students home.

Late Afternoon

Meet with a parent to talk about a student.
Grade homework and tests.
Work on tomorrow's teaching plan.
Leave school for the day at 4:30 PM.

Glossary

communicate—to pass knowledge.

electronic whiteboard—a special board used in the classroom that is able to connect with computers.

hearing impaired—a disability where a person is unable to hear as clearly as others.

license—a government certificate that allows a person to do something.

overhead projector—a machine that makes a picture big and shows it on a screen.

science—the study of nature and how Earth works.

teaching plans—an organized plan for what and when to teach certain information.

union—a group that helps workers gain fair pay and safe working conditions.

Did You Know?

🌐 In the past, a whole school was in one room. It was called a schoolhouse. There was one teacher for the school. Students from different grades were in the same class.

🌐 Anne Sullivan was a teacher called "the miracle worker." She had a student who could not hear or see. That student was Helen Keller. Anne helped Helen learn to communicate and become a role model for others.

On the Web

To learn more about teachers, visit ABDO Group online at **www.abdopublishing.com**. Web sites about teachers are featured on our Book Links page. These links are routinely monitored and updated to provide the most current information available.

Index

aides	15
class	4, 15, 19, 30
classroom	11, 23, 30
community	28
helping	4, 8, 11, 15
homework	7, 30
license	27
parents	11, 30
principal	12
problems	15
report cards	7
rules	11, 15
sign language	8
technology	20, 23, 30
tests	7, 30
tools	16, 19
training	27